© WORDS CONNECT
BY SANDEEP RAVIDUTT SHARMA

Table of Contents

Introduction IV

Words Connect..1

© WORDS CONNECT
BY SANDEEP RAVIDUTT SHARMA

Introduction

This book provides you with a **list of 100 motivational quotes and thoughts** focussing mainly on improving your wellness quotient. Be ready to use the right words which can create a healthy and positive energy field all around. It is the words that connects you to the world. Your choice of words may define your life path and guarantee support from others in your endeavour. Trust is lost within a minute the moment you utter words which are not to the liking of the other. At the same time, your words backed by your deeds builds trust and good relationships. You don't have to react against every action of the interacting person. Sometimes silence creates a better impact than your choice of words. I'm sure if you keep reading, referring, sharing these thoughts and quotes, you may derive inspiration and develop a good understanding of various perspectives and facts about life.

"Words connect you to the world of happiness or sorrow based on your choice."

I sincerely hope, you will find this book amazing, interesting, rejuvenating, unique and constant source of inspiration.

Thank You and Happy Reading.

WORDS CONNECT

© **WORDS CONNECT**
BY SANDEEP RAVIDUTT SHARMA

Paint your mind with amazing colours of joy.

© WORDS CONNECT
BY SANDEEP RAVIDUTT SHARMA

© Copyright 2018 Sandeep Ravidutt Sharma - All rights reserved.

In no way is it legal to reproduce, duplicate, or transmit any part of this document in either electronic means or in printed format. Recording of this publication is strictly prohibited and any storage of this document is not allowed unless with written permission from the publisher. All rights reserved. The information provided herein is stated to be truthful and consistent, in that any liability, in terms of inattention or otherwise, by any usage or abuse of any policies, processes, or directions contained within is the solitary and utter responsibility of the recipient reader. Under no circumstances will any legal responsibility or blame be held against the author / publisher for any reparation, damages, or monetary loss due to the information herein, either directly or indirectly. The author own all copyrights.

Legal Notice:
This book is copyright protected. This is only for personal use. You cannot amend, distribute, sell, use, quote or paraphrase any part or the content within this book without the consent of the author or copyright owner. Legal action will be pursued if this is breached.

Disclaimer Notice:
Please note the information contained within this book is for motivational, educational and knowledge sharing purpose only. Every attempt has been made to provide the reader accurate, up to date and reliable complete information. No warranties of any kind are expressed or implied. Readers acknowledge that the author is not engaging in the rendering of legal, financial, medical or professional advice. By reading this document, the reader agrees that under no circumstances the author / publisher is responsible for any losses, direct or indirect, which are incurred as a result of the use of information contained within this document, including, but not limited to, —errors, omissions, or inaccuracies.

If you have further questions, contact on
Tel: +919969256731
Email: sandeepraviduttsharma@gmail.com

© WORDS CONNECT
BY SANDEEP RAVIDUTT SHARMA

Dedication

This book is dedicated to Goddess Bhairavi. In the Hindu religion, the **Goddess Bhairavi** represents divine anger and wrath which is directed towards impurities within us as well as to the negative forces that obstructs our spiritual growth. **Bhairavi Mata** is also called as **Shubhamkari** and does good things. She is often depicted in images as holding a book, rosary and making abhaya and varada mudra with her hands. She is fiercely protective, lending us wisdom and power, steadiness and clarity. She personifies light and fire, supporting us to reveal what we keep hidden and inviting us to explore our hidden mind and any secret darkness.
 I hereby recite the following Bhairavi mool mantra...
"Om Hreem Bhairavi Kalaum Hreem Svaha"
And pray to Goddess Bhairavi for lending wisdom and power, steadiness and clarity in the life of my readers and the world. May Goddess Bhairavi protect us from negative forces along with removing impurities of our mind.

If the rope is pulled from both ends, it doesn't help anyone. But if the rope is held firm from both ends, it becomes a bridge for someone to cross the river.

The obstacles create illusions of failure. Be ready to cross them with your determined efforts and illusions are no more.

© **WORDS CONNECT**
BY SANDEEP RAVIDUTT SHARMA

World welcomes those who are determined to achieve.

© WORDS CONNECT
BY SANDEEP RAVIDUTT SHARMA

If you have the right attitude, challenges would turn into opportunities. Attitude matters.

Discipline is a must in all spheres of life, whether you are in a learning environment, workplace or at home.

With your positive attitude you can overcome the challenges in time.

© WORDS CONNECT
BY SANDEEP RAVIDUTT SHARMA

Amazing results very well know and appreciate the efforts that were really amazing.

Do not try to fast forward your present if you don't like it. You have to live it either with a smile or a frown. The choice is all yours.

Staying positive helps to scale the mountain of opportunities and reach the summit.

You can create your own destiny through self-belief.

Those who find ways to sneak into the future are losing their present. Live now.

Transformation of Sole to Soul takes a while and you are put to constant testing and hardship. Meditation can help you to gain soulful experiences.

Your voice will be heard if you manage to avoid the whisper and speak aloud.

God makes everything possible. Trust in the Lord and you can see all possibilities opening up in your life.

Believing in yourself helps you to believe others. With self-belief when your efforts are powered, you are bound to hit the target. Believing in the other motivates them to excel and produce results as per your plan.

© **WORDS CONNECT**
BY SANDEEP RAVIDUTT SHARMA

You only repent when your heart confirms that you were wrong but mind still believes you are right.

The seeker of truth needs a lot of patience and willpower while treading through hurdles and constraints laid all along the path.

Your positive response encourages the other to perform and deliver better.

Challenges unlock your strengths. Be grateful to the challenges you meet in your life path, they are the ones who will help you to discover and use your strengths to the optimum.

Arrogance fall is imminent while humility stands throughout.

You may deny your wrongdoing hundreds of time, but it is wise to accept it once forever. The choice is all yours.

The destination of everyone lies in different directions. We may meet and walk together for some distance in our life journey, so why not do it with a smile and joyfulness.

Same words spoken in changed tone and expression may mean differently to the recipients at different times.

Beware of man-made illusion. What you may see or hear may not be a complete truth.

Be in love rather than hate from a distance.

© **WORDS CONNECT**
BY SANDEEP RAVIDUTT SHARMA

The moment you accept that a given task is impossible to achieve. You are out of the competition. Exploring with the aim to achieve can make impossible things possible.

Believe in the best and it becomes reality.

© **WORDS CONNECT**
BY SANDEEP RAVIDUTT SHARMA

Clarity of responsibilities towards defined goals is mandatory for the individual and organisational growth.

Success isn't all about the money you make. It's more about how, where and when do you use this money.

Buying gifts makes you happy. Nature and the universe shower gifts on you every day without any cost. Be thankful to them. Trees smile and wave at you. Flowers make you feel good, cool breeze relaxes your body and soul, stars perform every night, the sun and Moon ensure that you enjoy your every moment in either golden or silver light. All these gifts are invaluable for you. Be ready to buy gifts for not just your near and dear ones but for total strangers and share happiness.

Sea inspires us again and again. Sea is so vast, cool and accommodates living and non-living beings. Sea inspires life, but it's also a reason for someone's death. Sea many a time recedes but at other times displays aggression and anger.

You need to dig hard to find the purpose of your life. Once you have found it then you have to pursue it with determined efforts.

Those who value real freedom can never enslave others.

Even fake emotions affect the emotional ones. Never play with emotions of the other.

Our likes and dislikes changes with the passage of time. Nothing is permanent in this universe. Keep Going is the mantra...

The leader shows the way when none exist for the other.

If you want others to notice you that how can you afford to stand far from the playing zone.

Words of wisdom are frozen in time and available for generations to come.

You should appreciate strongly whatever is right with encouraging words. But do criticize politely, whatever is wrong with noble intentions.

Don't dance to the tune of your desires else someday you may even have to learn how to walk again in life.

Go with the flow if there is no option but the moment you see a diversion pull back and choose your way.

As you try to take a dive into the deep ocean of thoughts, you are blessed with pearls of wisdom. These thoughts are valuable only when it is shared and used for the greater good.

Rub the shine of positivity by the grease of kind words.

Go slow when you don't know where your next step is about to fall.

Time flies for those who are watching it and not doing enough.

© **WORDS CONNECT**
BY SANDEEP RAVIDUTT SHARMA

Sing the song of your life playing with the strings of joy and sometimes getting hurt in the process.

If the story doesn't seem to end somewhere, it's not a story at all.

Health is wealth. Eat fresh fruits to live a healthy life.

Time invokes your desire and may also shatter your dreams.

Expose and replace the incompetent in time if you really want to win.

Just by tying the hands of the clock, you can't stop the forward march of time.

You don't need any pretext, to tell the truth. Truth is eternal and cannot hide for long.

Another day begins with the sunrise, turning a new page of your life. It's your day today, stay focused and give your best.

Attract divine music in your life, and you would no more crave for anything else in this world. Immerse your own self in music. It's enough to attain eternal happiness and infinite joy.

Seek blessings from elders instead of exploiting or extracting money.

You don't need to even touch the feet of those whom you respect if you touch their hearts with your good behaviour and kindness.

When you are busy driving things or people in your favour with good intentions don't bother about who is ganging up against you.

If you can forgive those who keep hurting you. You will be at peace.

You need to wait when it's matter of principle and the right process needs to be followed.

Patience can dethrone the cruellest ruler.

You just can't stop the rain by opening an umbrella. It only helps you to save yourself from getting wet. Life challenges will keep raining, use your knowledge and creativity to convert them into opportunities.

Bargaining in business and your life indicates that both parties are not sure of the actual worth.

© **WORDS CONNECT**
BY SANDEEP RAVIDUTT SHARMA

Your perspective decides your response to a given situation or opportunity.

Give your helping hand to the one in need. It is worth more than your riches.

Difficulties in life lead to innovative solutions.

You feel happy when you get what you want, but happiness multiplies when you get the unexpected. Because it's purely God's wish which reigns supreme.

Don't let your mind pull your heart just because you want to win.

© **WORDS CONNECT**
BY SANDEEP RAVIDUTT SHARMA

Success and failure are two sides of the life coin. One gives joy and the other fills sadness. The choice is all yours...whether you want to go overboard after you succeed or learn lessons out of your failure...

Writing a letter is not just about arranging words and sentences but it's more about how you can convey your message effectively without the opportunity to physically display your expressions and emotions.

You create your own worth which gets value tag from others.

Free up your mind if you have something to say. If no one listens you can talk to the almighty God when you pray.

© **WORDS CONNECT**
BY SANDEEP RAVIDUTT SHARMA

Roses and Thorns come in the same package whether you like it or not.

Don't just argue for the sake of winning or dominating the other person but essentially for making the other person understand your perspective. One-sided arguments lead to damaging your relationship.

© **WORDS CONNECT**
BY SANDEEP RAVIDUTT SHARMA

Life awaits the fulfilment of your dreams. Don't just dream but take the first step towards achieving the same.

Time creates memories for you, and it may steal your memory as well.

© WORDS CONNECT
BY SANDEEP RAVIDUTT SHARMA

When you don't feel like doing anything. Nothing motivates you. Stay low and relax for a while. Look for inspiration in books, good deeds and rejuvenate your mind again. Kickstart your self-motivating engine.

The style is important but simplicity is forever.

Welcome positive thoughts without even thinking to strike the negative ones.

You may take a big decision once a while and fail. Alternatively, you can take a number of small decisions and succeed one day.

© **WORDS CONNECT**
BY SANDEEP RAVIDUTT SHARMA

Your helping hand can make a person and create the feel-good environment for you.

The world is too small, and people meet again even after saying Goodbye.

You will know about your potential only when challenges push you against the wall.

When you can't help someone economically at least offer kind and motivational words.

© **WORDS CONNECT**
BY SANDEEP RAVIDUTT SHARMA

If you are good enough, you can even sell your dreams by converting it into a story worth reading.

Sometimes doing nothing helps you to regain your focus and remove clutter from your choked mind

Get inspiration from flowers. They have such a short life but are never tired of smiling.

Sea exhibits both kinds of extreme behavior every day. There are times when the mood is dipped in anger sauce and Sea wants to move anything in its path. At other times Sea is in withdrawal mode marked with complete silence. Mood swings are common among humans and can very well influence one's bid for success.

Have faith in your own abilities instead of awaiting certification from others.

Good deeds may not make you wealthy but definitely make you more worthy than the richest man on earth.

Spend more time on handling the major issues but never ignore the minor ones.

The world inspires me to give my best. That doesn't mean I have to focus on the world and not my performance.

© **WORDS CONNECT**
BY SANDEEP RAVIDUTT SHARMA

Start your day with a prayer and see how the day turns out to be.

Fulfil your ambitions with your hard work and innovative ideas.

If somebody yells at you, don't yell back but ensure complete attention to what the other person is trying to communicate. It's difficult no doubt to practice this than simply preach. But still, give your best to keep patience and see the effect on the other person. I'm sure your patience will win and fire will be doused off automatically.

The healthy relationship is not a myth but reality provided good understanding prevails at all ends.

Aspire to win.

Advice remains advice when there is no action supporting it.

If you are not being heard, then it is wise to speak through your silence.

Time never stops and is constantly on the run. You can't match pace with time unless you are also interested in running throughout your life and never relax.

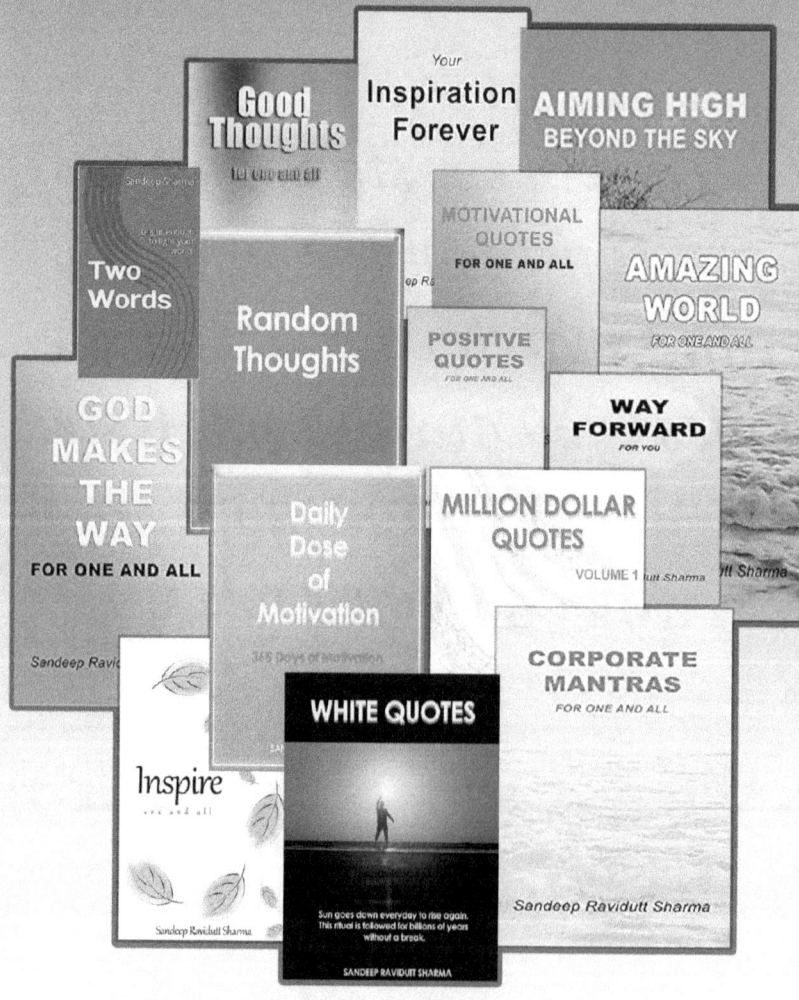

www.ingramcontent.com/pod-product-compliance
Lightning Source LLC
Chambersburg PA
CBHW070804220526
45466CB00002B/533